The Nutella Connoisseur Cookbook

Forty Mouth-Watering Recipes for the
Nutella People

By

Angel Burns

License Notices

This book or parts thereof might not be reproduced in any format for personal or commercial use without the written permission of the author. Possession and distribution of this book by any means without said permission is prohibited by law.

All content is for entertainment purposes and the author accepts no responsibility for any damages, commercially or personally, caused by following the content.

Table of Contents

Simple & Delicious Nutella Recipes

HHHHHHHHHHHHHHHHHHHHHHHHHHHHHHHHHHHHHHHHH

Recipe 1: Nutella Cheese Ball

A delicious savory appetizer or party crowd pleaser.

Serving Sizes: 12

Preparation Time: 1hour 10mins

Cook Time: N/A

Total Cooking Time: 1hour 10mins

Ingredient List:

- 8 ounces cream cheese (softened)
- ½ cup powdered sugar
- ½ teaspoons vanilla essence
- ¼ teaspoons salt
- ⅓ cup Nutella
- 1 cup mini chocolate chips

HHHHHHHHHHHHHHHHHHHHHHHHHHHHHHHHHHH

Instructions:

1. In a bowl, combine the cream cheese with the sugar, vanilla essence and salt until silky smooth.

2. Add the Nutella, and stir until incorporated.

3. Put the mixture in the center of a piece of kitchen wrap approximately 18" in length.

4. Form the wrap around the mixture to make a ball.

5. Twist the top of the plastic to seal slightly and transfer to the freezer for 60 minutes.

6. Re-form the mixture into a round ball, and return to the freezer.

7. When ready to serve, roll the ball in mini choc chips.

Recipe 2: Spicy Chocolate Cupcakes with Nutella Chili Chocolate Ganache & Chili Cream Cheese Frosting

These are not your average cupcakes! Impress family and friends with sophisticated spiced chocolate sponge filled with rich ganache and topped with lashing of fluffy cream cheese frosting.

Serving Sizes: 12

Preparation Time: 40mins

Cook Time: 25mins

Total Cooking Time: 1hour 5mins

Ingredient List:

Cupcakes:

- 2 cups cake flour (plus extra for tin)
- ½ cup unsweetened cocoa powder
- 1 cup sugar
- ½ teaspoons ground red pepper flakes
- 2 teaspoons baking powder
- ⅔ cup vegetable oil
- 1 teaspoon vanilla
- 2 large eggs
- 1 cup milk

Ganache:

- ⅔ cup heavy cream
- 6 ounces dark chocolate (chopped)
- ½ cup Nutella
- 3 tablespoons unsalted butter
- 1 teaspoon ancho chili powder

Frosting:

- 1 teaspoon ancho chili powder
- ⅛ teaspoons cayenne pepper
- ½ teaspoons ground cinnamon
- 2 cups powdered sugar
- 1 package (8 ounces) cream cheese (room temperature)
- 8 tablespoons unsalted butter (softened)
- ½ teaspoons vanilla essence
- Cinnamon sticks (to decorate)

HHHHHHHHHHHHHHHHHHHHHHHHHHHHHHHHHHHHH

Instructions:

1. For the cupcakes: Preheat the main oven to 375 degrees F. Lightly grease and dust 24 muffin cups with flour.

2. In a bowl, mix and sift the flour, along with the cocoa, sugar, pepper flakes and baking powder.

3. Add the oil followed by the vanilla, eggs, and milk, while beating on low speed in a stand mixer for 30 seconds, remembering to scrape down the sides of the bowl as needed. Continue to beat for between 7-8 minutes at moderate speed.

4. Pour the cake batter into the muffin cups.

5. Bake in the preheated oven for 18-20 minutes, or until the top of the cupcakes are springy to the touch.

6. Remove the cupcakes from the oven and allow to cool while remaining in their pans for several minutes, after which remove and transfer to a wire baking rack to cool.

7. Using an apple corer, remove the very middle of the cupcake to make space for the filling.

8. To prepare the ganache: In a small pan bring the cream to boil. Remove the pan from the heat and add the chocolate followed by the Nutella and butter and allow to sit for 2-3 minutes.

9. Stir the mixture slowly until the ingredients are combined.

10. Stir in the chili, adding additional chili to increase the spiciness.

11. Allow the ganache to cool for half an hour before filling each cupcake.

12. Using a teaspoon, fill each cupcake with ganache until it reaches the rim of the top of each cake.

13. You can now frost the cupcakes.

14. For the frosting sift together the chili powder together with the cayenne pepper, cinnamon, and powdered sugar and set to one side.

15. Using a stand mixer, fitted with a paddle attachment, on moderate speed, beat the cream cheese together with the butter for 4-5 minutes.

16. Stir in the vanilla essence.

17. Add the sugar mixture to the cream cheese mixture and mix to combine.

18. Pipe the cupcakes with the frosting and decorate with a stick of cinnamon.

Recipe 3: Nutella Crêpes with Coconut Milk & Candied Double-Smoked Bacon

It's surprising how good candied bacon tastes alongside sweet ingredients. These crepes are truly delicious for breakfast, lunch or as a snack.

Serving Sizes: 4

Preparation Time: 10mins

Cook Time: 20mins

Total Cooking Time: 30mins

Ingredient List:

- 4 slices double smoked bacon
- 1 small jar golden syrup
- 17½ ounces milk
- 1½ ounces butter (plus extra for cooking)
- 8¾ ounces flour
- 3 medium eggs (beaten)
- 1 pinch of fine salt
- 1 (13 ounce) small jar Nutella
- 1 (13 ounce) can coconut milk

HHHHHHHHHHHHHHHHHHHHHHHHHHHHHHHHHHHHH

Instructions:

1. Preheat the main oven to 375 degrees F.

2. Arrange the slices of bacon on a rack set on top of a baking sheet. Lightly brush the bacon with syrup. Roast the bacon in the oven for 15-20 minutes, or until crispy. Set to one side.

3. In the meantime, in a microwave-safe bowl, heat the milk together with the butter in 30-second intervals, until the butter melts. Allow to cool.

4. Add the flour, eggs, and salt, continually stirring until the mixture is silky. Heat a large frying pan over moderate heat.

5. Melt a small amount of the butter in the pan, swirling so that it evenly coats the pan.

6. With a ladle, add approximately ¼ of the crepe batter, swirling so that it evenly coats the base of the pan.

7. As soon as most of it has set, loosen the edges of the crepe and flip it over, to allow the rest to cook. Repeat the process with the remaining batter.

8. Spoon the Nutella into each of the crepes, folding each crepe in half to form a triangular shape. Warm for 40-50 seconds in the microwave.

9. Top with coconut milk and sprinkle with candied bacon.

Recipe 4: African Chicken Nutella Stew

An African inspired chunky chicken and veggie stew flavored with curry and hazelnut.

Serving Sizes: 4

Preparation Time: 10mins

Cook Time: 1hour

Total Cooking Time: 1hour 10mins

Ingredient List:

- 1 tablespoon butter
- 1 tablespoon olive oil
- 4 skinless, boneless chicken breasts
- 2 garlic cloves (peeled, chopped)
- ½ onion (peeled, cut into thin wedges)
- 4 large potatoes (chopped)
- 2 carrots (chopped)
- 10 ounces chicken stock
- 5 ounces water
- 1 tablespoon curry
- 1 tomato (seeded, diced)
- ½ cup Nutella
- Fresh cilantro (chopped)
- 2 tablespoons plain flour
- 2 tablespoons water

HHHHHHHHHHHHHHHHHHHHHHHHHHHHHHHHHHHHHH

Instructions:

1. In a large pan, heat the butter and olive oil over moderate heat. Add the chicken breasts and cook until lightly brown. Add the garlic, followed by the onion, and fry until softened.

2. Add the potatoes, carrots, followed by the chicken stock, water, curry, tomato, Nutella, and cilantro.

3. Simmer for half an hour or until the veggies are fork tender.

4. Combine the flour with the water and stir to incorporate.

5. Increase the heat under the pan and add the flour-water mixture, this will help to thicken the stew.

6. Cook until sufficiently thickened and serve with crusty bread.

No results found for the text you pasted (193 words), on 8 Jan 2018 at 12:40 GMT. More information

Recipe 5: Venison Nutella Jumbo Meatballs

These man-sized meatballs are super juicy and moist thanks to the rich venison mince and gooey Nutella center.

Serving Sizes: 5 (2 large meatballs per serving)

Preparation Time: 15mins

Cook Time: 35mins

Total Cooking Time: 1hour 50mins

Ingredient List:

- 1½ pounds venison mince
- 4 tablespoons game seasoning mix
- 6-7 tablespoons Nutella (still in the jar)
- BBQ sauce (for basting)
- 2 tablespoons hazelnuts (chopped)

HHHHHHHHHHHHHHHHHHHHHHHHHHHHHHHHHHHHHH

Instructions:

1. Using your hands, combine the mince and seasoning in a large bowl.

2. Roll 10 equally-sized balls of mince and flatten them with the palm of your hand to make patties.

3. Use a small melon baller to scoop balls of Nutella from the jar, one at a time. Place on small ball of Nutella into the center of each venison patty.

4. Shape the mince around the Nutella to form large meatballs.

5. Chill the meatballs for an hour, until firm.

6. Preheat your grill to around 350 degrees F, for the indirect cooking.

7. Arrange the meatballs on the grill and cook for 20-25 minutes with the lid down.

8. Brush the meatballs with BBQ sauce and cook for a final 10 minutes.

9. Transfer to a serving plate and sprinkle over the chopped hazelnuts.

Recipe 6: Bacon & Nutella Soufflé

Crumbled bacon inside a soft soufflé is a winning combination of texture and flavor.

Serving Sizes: 2

Preparation Time: 15mins

Cook Time: 15mins

Total Cooking Time: 30mins

Ingredient List:

- 1 teaspoon butter (softened)
- ½ teaspoons sugar
- 1 cup Nutella
- ¼ cup heavy cream
- 1 medium egg yolk
- ½ teaspoons vanilla essence
- Pinch salt
- 3 medium egg whites
- 1 tablespoon sugar
- 6 strips bacon (cooked, crumbled)

HHHHHHHHHHHHHHHHHHHHHHHHHHHHHHHHHHHHHHH

Instructions:

1. Preheat the main oven to 425 degrees F. Lightly grease 2 (6 ounce) ramekins with softened butter and lightly sprinkle with ½ teaspoons of sugar.

2. In a large mixing bowl, and using a hand mixer whip together the Nutella, heavy cream, followed by the egg yolk, vanilla essence, and a pinch of salt. Mix until silky smooth.

3. Pour the egg whites into the mixing bowl of an electric mixer and on a high speed, whip.

4. A little at a time, and while continuing to whip, add 1 tablespoon of sugar. Continue whipping until stiff peaks begin to form.

5. Pour the egg whites over the Nutella mixture and very gently fold together. Once almost completely incorporated, fold in the cooked, crumbled bacon.

6. Pour the batter into the prepared, lightly greased ramekins.

7. Transfer to the middle rack of the preheated oven for 15 minutes.

No results found for the text you pasted (216 words), on 8 Jan 2018 at 12:42 GMT

Recipe 7: Three Cheese French Toast

Nutella is the perfect breakfast and especially tasty with three different types of cheese.

Serving Sizes: 2

Preparation Time: 10mins

Cook Time: 15mins

Total Cooking Time: 25mins

Ingredient List:

- 2 medium eggs
- 1 cup unsweetened almond milk
- ¼ teaspoons vanilla essence
- 2 tablespoons agave nectar
- 4 (1") slices challah
- 3 tablespoons part-skim ricotta cheese
- 1 tablespoon goat cheese
- 2 tablespoons Nutella
- 1 tablespoon butter
- 6 square, thin slices extra sharp cheddar cheese

HHHHHHHHHHHHHHHHHHHHHHHHHHHHHHHHHHHHH

Instructions:

1. Preheat the main oven to 350 degrees F.

2. In a mixing bowl, whisk the eggs together with the almond milk, vanilla essence, and agave nectar.

3. Arrange the 4 slices of challah in a large casserole dish. Pour the egg mixture over the challah, gently pressing them so that they absorb the mixture. Set to one side.

4. Meanwhile, whisk together both the ricotta cheese along with the goat cheese and Nutella and put to one side.

Recipe 8: Bacon, Nutella, and Onion Burger Relish

A sweet and savory relish that will give your grilled food the wow factor.

Serving Sizes: 18-20

Preparation Time: 15mins

Cook Time: 2hours

Total Cooking Time: 2hours 15mins

Ingredient List:

- 2 pounds bacon rashers (chopped)
- 2 large sweet onions (peeled, chopped)
- 4 cloves garlic (minced)
- 1 cup cider vinegar
- 2 cups fresh strong-brewed coffee (cooled
- ½ cup Nutella
- 1 cup organic pineapple juice (unsweetened)
- ¼ cup canned crushed pineapple (juice drained)
- ½ teaspoons cinnamon
- 2 tablespoons light brown sugar
- ¼ teaspoons black pepper
- ⅓ cup peach nectar

HHHHHHHHHHHHHHHHHHHHHHHHHHHHHHHHHHHHHH

Instructions:

1. Fry the bacon in a large stockpot over medium heat, when browned remove from the pan and set aside on a paper-towel-lined plate.

2. Drain away all but 3 tablespoons of the bacon fat.

3. Add the onion to the pot, sauté for 5 minutes, until soft. Next, add the minced garlic and cook for 60 seconds. Place the bacon back in the pan.

4. Pour in the vinegar, coffee, Nutella, pineapple juice, crushed pineapple, cinnamon, brown sugar, and black pepper. Bring to a boil, then turn the heat down low and simmer for 45 minutes. Take off the heat and allow to cool a little.

5. Transfer the mixture to a food processor* and pulse until chopped.

6. Pour the mixture back into the stockpot and bring to the boil. Turn down to a simmer and cook for 15 minutes before stirring in the peach nectar. Simmer for a final half an hour until thick.

7. Allow to cool to room temperature before spooning into clean airtight re-sealable jars**.

*In batches if necessary.

**Keep chilled.

Recipe 9: Stracchino & Nutella Ciabatta

Stracchino is a variety of Italian cow's milk cheese. It is soft and super creamy, with a delicate and mild flavor which is perfectly combined with the nutty sweetness of Nutella.

Serving Sizes: 4

Preparation Time: 5mins

Cook Time: 5mins

Total Cooking Time: 10mins

Ingredient List:

- 8 tablespoons Nutella
- 8 thick slices ciabatta
- 8 (½") thick slices Stracchino cheese
- ¼ cup butter (melted)

HHHHHHHHHHHHHHHHHHHHHHHHHHHHHHHHHHHHH

Instructions:

1. Evenly spread 2 tablespoons of Nutella over 4 slices ciabatta, then top with 2 thick slices of cheese. Make 4 sandwiches with the remaining bread slices.

2. Over moderate to hot heat, heat a gas grill.

3. Brush both sides of each sandwich with the melted butter.

4. Grill each of the sandwiches until golden on both sides, this will take around 2-4 minutes on each side.

Recipe 10: Bacon, Peanut Butter, and Nutella Breakfast Crescent Rolls

Get your day off to a great start with these buttery, flaky rolls filled with the holy trinity of breakfast foods; bacon, peanut butter, and Nutella!

Serving Sizes: 8

Preparation Time: 10mins

Cook Time: 20mins

Total Cooking Time: 30mins

Ingredient List:

- 1 (8 ounce) tube crescent roll dough
- 8 teaspoons Nutella
- 8 teaspoons smooth peanut butter
- 8 rashers cooked crispy bacon (crumbled)
- Confectioner's sugar

HHHHHHHHHHHHHHHHHHHHHHHHHHHHHHHHHHHHHHHH

Instructions:

1. Preheat the main oven to 350 degrees F.

2. Separate the dough into the 8 pre-marked dough triangles.

3. Spread 1 teaspoon each of Nutella and peanut butter on each triangle and sprinkle with crumbled bacon.

4. Roll up the triangles, starting from the widest end.

5. Arrange the rolls on a cookie sheet.

6. Place in the oven and bake for just over 15 minutes.

7. Dust with sugar and serve warm or at room temperature.

Recipe 11: Steak with Chocolate, Hazelnut and Pepper Sauce

Tender steak with chocolate and hazelnut sauce may not seem like an obvious choice but once you try it there's no going back.

Serving Sizes: 4

Preparation Time: 15mins

Cook Time: 15mins

Total Cooking Time: 50mins

Ingredient List:

- 3 tablespoons sea salt
- 1 pound skirt steak
- 1 yellow chili pepper
- 2 tablespoons olive oil
- 1 cup beef stock
- 1 tablespoon Nutella
- Freshly ground black pepper
- ⅓ cup dry Spanish Jerez (sherry)
- 1tablespoon flour
- 1 tablespoon brewed coffee
- 1 teaspoon raw cacao
- 1 pinch dried oregano
- 1 teaspoon butter

HHHHHHHHHHHHHHHHHHHHHHHHHHHHHHHHHHHHHH

Instructions:

1. Rub the sea salt into the steak and set to one side to rest for 15 minutes.

2. In the meanwhile, in a skillet, dry roast the chili pepper on high heat until the pepper begins to blister, this will take 2-3 minutes.

3. Remove the pepper from the skillet and transfer to a small bowl, pour sufficient boiling water into the bowl to cover. Allow to rest for 2-3 minutes. As soon as the chili is soft, cut it across its length, deseed and devein.

4. In a food processor or blender combine the ¼ cup of stock with the chili and Nutella and set to one side.

5. Lightly shake the salt off the steak and brush with 1 tablespoon of oil, and season with freshly ground black pepper.

6. Pan sear or grill the steak in a hot pan for approximately 2-3 minutes per side.

7. When cooked to your liking, remove the steak from the grill and set to rest on a dinner plate and loosely tent to keep warm.

8. Using the sherry, deglaze the pan, and add the olive oil, beef drippings, and ¾ cup of stock. Add the flour to the pan and whisk well to incorporate. Continually stirring for 60 seconds.

9. Next, add the Nutella-chili liquid along with the brewed coffee and raw cacao. Whisk well to incorporate until you achieve the desired thickness.

10. Scatter with oregano, and stir to combine.

11. Lastly, add the butter to give the sauce a gloss.

12. Cut the steak across the grain, and serve with some of the sauce over the top of the steak.

Recipe 12: Brie, Nutella, and Basil Panini

It's amazing how versatile Nutella is. Here, served with salty Brie and basil it makes the perfect savory panini.

Serving Sizes: 6

Preparation Time: 5mins

Cook Time: 15mins

Total Cooking Time: 20mins

Ingredient List:

- 12 slices multigrain panini bread
- 6 ounces Nutella
- 12 ounces Brie cheese (sliced)
- Handful fresh basil leaves
- Butter

HHHHHHHHHHHHHHHHHHHHHHHHHHHHHHHHHHHHHH

Instructions:

1. Preheat your Panini grill.

2. Spread one side of each slice of bread with Nutella.

3. Top with 2 ounces of Brie and 2-3 leaves of basil.

4. Top with another slice of multigrain bread to make a sandwich.

5. Butter both sides of the sandwich for grilling and in the panini maker, grill until the bread is lightly golden and the Brie melting.

6. Repeat the process until all of the ingredients are used.

No results found for the text you pasted (132 words), on 8 Jan 2018 at 12:49 GMT.

Recipe 13: Spicy Nutella and Cayenne Pepper Truffles

Nutella truffles spiced with cayenne are a decadent and indulgent after dinner treat to enjoy with coffee.

Serving Sizes: 25

Preparation Time: 15mins

Cook Time: 5mins

Total Cooking Time: 2hours

Ingredient List:

- 1 (13 ounce) jar Nutella
- 2 (3½ ounce) bars 70% cocoa dark chocolate (divided)
- 1 tablespoon butter
- 1 teaspoon cayenne pepper

HHHHHHHHHHHHHHHHHHHHHHHHHHHHHHHHHHHHHH

Instructions:

1. Melt together the Nutella, half the dark chocolate, and all of the butter using a double boiler. Stir well until the mixture starts to come away from the side of the bowl.

2. Shape the mixture into a mound and return to the bowl. Cover with kitchen wrap and chill in the fridge for a minimum of 60 minutes, or until the firm enough to work with.

3. Roll the mixture into 25 walnut sized ball shapes,

4. Should the mixture become too sticky or soft, return to the fridge to chill more.

5. Transfer the chocolate balls to the freezer for 15-20 minutes.

6. In the meanwhile, melt the remaining chocolate in the double boiler and remove from the heat.

7. Using a cocktail stick, spear each one of the frozen balls and dip in the melted chocolate.

8. Slowly turn the cocktail stick, allowing any excess chocolate to drip off.

9. Sprinkle the truffle with cayenne pepper.

10. As soon as the chocolate sets and firms remove the cocktail stick and place the truffles on a tray lined with parchment paper.

11. Repeat the process with the remaining chocolate balls.

12. Allow the truffles to rest at room temperature for 20 minutes, then transfer to the fridge until ready to serve.

Recipe 14: Nutella & Goat Cheese Melt

Goat cheese pairs exceptionally well with Nutella to make a sweet and savory lunchtime melted sandwich.

Serving Sizes: 4

Preparation Time: 4mins

Cook Time: 5mins

Total Cooking Time: 9mins

Ingredient List:

- 8 tablespoons Nutella
- 4 ounces fresh goat cheese (room temperature)
- 2 tablespoons butter (room temperature)
- 8 slices ¼" thick country bread

HHHHHHHHHHHHHHHHHHHHHHHHHHHHHHHHHHHHHHH

Instructions:

1. In a small mixing bowl, add the Nutella to the goat cheese and stir to combine.

2. Butter one side of each side of the 8 slices of bread.

3. Spread the Nutella-cheese mixture on the unbuttered side of each slice of bread.

4. Make 4 sandwiches, buttered side facing upwards.

5. On a moderately hot grill, grill the sandwiches until the bread is golden, and the cheese melting, this will take around 4-5 minutes for each sandwich.

6. Serve at once.

Recipe 15: Black Bean, Pepitas, and Nutella Spread

A versatile spread or dip with a hint of sweetness. It's a little spicy and has a depth of flavor courtesy of the cacao powder.

Serving Sizes: 4-6

Preparation Time: 15mins

Cook Time: 5mins

Total Cooking Time: 20mins

Ingredient List:

- 2 tablespoons pepitas
- 3 teaspoons avocado oil (divided)
- ¼ teaspoons cumin
- 1 small shallot (diced)
- 2 cloves garlic (peeled, chopped)
- 1 (14 ounce) can black beans (fully drained)
- 1 tablespoon chunky peanut butter
- 1 chipotle pepper in adobo
- 1½ tablespoons Nutella
- Pinch of salt
- 2 tablespoons freshly squeezed lime juice
- 1 teaspoon raw cacao powder
- ½ avocado (peeled, pitted)
- Chopped cilantro (to garnish)

HHHHHHHHHHHHHHHHHHHHHHHHHHHHHHHHHHHHHH

Instructions:

1. Dry roast the pepitas in a frying pan over moderate heat until toasted, for 60 seconds, until you hear popping. Frequently stirring, to avoid burning. Take off the heat and put to one side.

2. Using the same pan, heat 1 teaspoon of avocado oil on moderately low heat and add the cumin, followed by the diced shallots, sauté until softened.

3. Add the chopped garlic and stir for 1 minute. Turn the heat off and add the black beans.

4. Using the back of a spoon, mash the beans into the shallot-garlic mixture in the pan and set to one side.

5. Add 75% of the bean mixture to a food blender followed by the peanut butter, roasted pepitas, chipotle in adobo, Nutella, salt, freshly squeezed lime juice and the remaining avocado oil.

6. Next, add the cacao powder and avocado to the blender and briefly process.

7. Taste, add more salt or Nutella according to your preference.

8. Add the remaining black bean mixture and stir to incorporate.

9. Serve garnished with chopped cilantro.

Recipe 16: Spicy 'n Sweet Nutella Coated Bacon

Thought bacon couldn't get any better? Then wait until you try this spicy n sweet bacon with chili brown sugar seasoning and a crunchy Nutella coating.

Serving Sizes: 2-3

Preparation Time: 4mins

Cook Time: 6mins

Total Cooking Time: 10mins

Ingredient List:

- 1 teaspoon chili powder
- 1 tablespoon brown sugar
- 1 teaspoon black pepper
- Nonstick spray
- 6 thick-cut rashers bacon
- 3 tablespoons Nutella
- Sea salt flakes

HHHHHHHHHHHHHHHHHHHHHHHHHHHHHHHHHHHHHHH

Instructions:

1. Preheat the main oven to 375 degrees F.

2. In a bowl combine the chili powder, sugar, and black pepper. Set aside.

3. Spritz a baking sheet with nonstick spray.

4. Place the rashers of bacon on the baking sheet and bake in the oven for approximately 7-9 minutes.

5. Turn the rashers over and sprinkle with the spice mix.

6. Take out of the oven and set to one side to cool.

7. Heat the Nutella in the microwave for 15-17 seconds, until runny.

8. Use a pastry brush to coat the cooled bacon with the Nutella on both sides.

9. Place the coated bacon on a sheet of parchment and chill for 1-2 hours, until the coating has set.

10. Sprinkle with sea salt flakes and enjoy!

Recipe 17: Boozy Stew Stuffed Potatoes

A rich and hearty beef stew, enhanced by the nutty sweetness of Nutella is stuffed into fluffy baked potatoes for the ultimate taste sensation.

Serving Sizes: 4

Preparation Time: 15mins

Cook Time: 2hours

Total Cooking Time: 2hours 15mins

Ingredient List:

- 2 tablespoons olive oil
- 1½ pounds stewing beef (chopped into chunks)
- 1 tablespoon flour
- Kosher salt and black pepper
- 1 white onion (peeled, chopped)
- 2 garlic cloves (minced)
- 1 tablespoon tomato puree
- 1 chipotle in adobo sauce (finely chopped)
- ½ teaspoons ground cumin
- ⅛ teaspoons ground cloves
- ¼ teaspoons paprika
- ¼ teaspoons chili powder
- ⅛ teaspoons allspice
- ½ teaspoons ground cinnamon
- ½ cup dry red wine
- 8 ounces dark beer
- 1 cup beef stock
- 2 ounces Nutella
- 4 medium potatoes (scrubbed)

HHHHHHHHHHHHHHHHHHHHHHHHHHHHHHHHHHHHHH

Instructions:

1. Heat half of the oil in a heavy saucepan over moderately high heat.

2. Toss the beef in the flour along with a little salt and black pepper.

3. Add the coated beef to the pan and cook until browned. Take the beef out of the pot and set aside.

4. Add the remaining oil to the pan along with the onions, cook for several minutes until soft.

5. Add the garlic, cooking for 60 seconds before adding the tomato paste along with the chipotle, cumin, cloves, paprika, chili powder, allspice, and cinnamon.

6. Pour in the red wine and using a wooden spoon loosen any bits from the bottom of the pan.

7. Add the beer, beef stock, and set-aside beef to the pan. Stir, and then add the Nutella. Keep stirring until the Nutella melts into the stew.

8. Bring to a boil, then turn down to a simmer. Cover and cook for an hour.

9. Remove the lid, stir and cook for a final 30 minutes.

10. Preheat the main oven to 375 degrees F.

11. In the meantime, wrap the potatoes in foil and bake in the oven for an hour.

12. Slice the top off each potato and scoop out a little fluffy potato from the center. Spoon stew into each potato and serve!

Recipe 18: Spanish Sausage and Nutella Sandwich

Smokey paprika, salty chorizo fuses with the nutty, sweet Nutella to deliver the perfect Spanish inspired snack.

Serving Sizes: 4

Preparation Time: 10mins

Cook Time: 15mins

Total Cooking Time:25mins

Ingredient List:

- 8 (1-1½" thick) slices sourdough bread
- Virgin olive oil
- Cured Spanish chorizo (cut into 2" slices)
- 2 garlic cloves (peeled, cut in half)
- 3 tablespoons Nutella
- Sea salt (to season)
- Fresh paprika

HHHHHHHHHHHHHHHHHHHHHHHHHHHHHHHHHHHHHHH

Instructions:

1. Lightly toast the sourdough bread and put to one side to cool.

2. In a small pan, heat a drop of oil, add the slices of chorizo and fry until sufficiently cooked. Reserve the oil.

3. Rub one side of each piece of toast with the cut side of a fresh garlic half and drizzle with olive oil.

4. Using a pastry cutter, cut the bread into circles.

5. Spread a fine layer of Nutella over the top of each circle and scatter with a pinch of sea salt. Arrange the thin slices of cooked chorizo on half of the slices.

6. Top with a slice of Nutella buttered toast.

7. Pop under the grill quickly to re-heat and drizzle with more olive oil and sprinkle with fresh paprika.

Recipe 19: Brie, Pear, Fig & Nutella Grilled Sandwich

Chocolate and cheese are an amazing sweet and savory combination. Try it; we know you will agree.

Serving Sizes: 2

Preparation Time: 5mins

Cook Time: 10mins

Total Cooking Time: 15mins

Ingredient List:

- 2 tablespoons salted butter
- 4 thick slices white bread
- 3 tablespoons Nutella (divided)
- 4 ounces double or triple cream brie (cut into thin, long strips)
- 1 Bartlett pear (thinly sliced)
- ⅓ cup dried figs (sliced into flat strips)

HHHHHHHHHHHHHHHHHHHHHHHHHHHHHHHHHHHHHH

Instructions:

1. Over moderately low heat, warm a skillet.

2. Spread ½ tablespoons of butter on each of the 4 slices of bread, on one side only.

3. Add 2 slices of bread, butter side facing down, to the skillet.

4. Spread 1½ tablespoons of Nutella on both slices of bread in the skillet.

5. Top the bread with an equal portion of Brie.

6. Arrange the slices of pear and dried figs on top of the Brie.

7. Lay the remaining 2 slices of bread, unbuttered side facing down, on top of the figs, to form 2 sandwiches.

8. Carefully, brown the bottom slice of bread, until crisp and browned.

9. Flip the sandwiches over, without allowing any filling to leak out.

10. Brown the bread, until lightly golden. The Brie should be gooey and melted.

11. Remove from the pan and enjoy.

Recipe 20: Smoky Chili con Carne

Nutella gives this family classic, chili con carne a hazelnut twist

Serving Sizes: 6

Preparation Time: 10mins

Cook Time: 45mins

Total Cooking Time: 55mins

Ingredient List:

- 2 tablespoons avocado oil
- 1 shallot (diced)
- 2 stalks celery (diced)
- 1 carrot (peeled, diced)
- 2 bay leaves
- ½ teaspoons ground cumin
- ¼ teaspoons celery salt
- ¼ teaspoons smoked Spanish paprika
- 3 garlic cloves (peeled, minced)
- 1 pound ground beef
- 6 tablespoons tomato paste
- ½ teaspoons salt
- 1¼ tablespoons Nutella
- 2 cups beef broth
- 1 tablespoon Worcestershire sauce
- ½ chipotle in adobe sauce (seeded, finely chopped)
- 6 white button mushrooms (diced)
- 1 (14 ounce) can red kidney beans
- ¼ red pepper (diced)
- Sour cream (to serve)
- Tortillas (to serve)

Instructions:

1. Heat the avocado oil in a heavy-bottomed pot over moderate heat.

2. Add the diced shallot, followed by the celery, and carrot and fry until softened, while occasionally stirring.

3. Once sizzling, add the bay leaves, ground cumin, celery salt and paprika, stirring for approximately 30 seconds.

4. Add the minced garlic to combine, and then add the beef. Stir to cook through until browned.

5. Next, add the tomato paste, salt, and Nutella together with the broth, Worcestershire sauce and chipotle. Stir well to incorporate.

6. As soon as the ingredients are incorporated, add the mushrooms, red kidney beans, and red pepper.

7. Turn the heat down to low, cover with a lid, and allow to simmer for half an hour, while occasionally stirring.

8. The veggies will be soft and the chili sauce reduced.

9. To thin the chili's consistency, add a drop of water and season to taste.

10. Serve with sour cream and tortillas.

Recipe 21: Butternut Squash Ravioli with Nutella Sauce

A meat-free ravioli is the perfect midweek family meal.

Serving Sizes: 6

Preparation Time: 30mins

Cook Time: 10mins

Total Cooking Time: 40mins

Ingredient List:

Nutella Sauce:

- 4 tablespoons butter
- 2 tablespoons flour
- 2 tablespoons Nutella
- 1 teaspoon cinnamon
- 1 teaspoon nutmeg
- 1 cup whipping cream

Butternut Squash Ravioli:

- 1 cup butternut squash (cooked, mashed)
- ½ teaspoons salt
- ½ teaspoons freshly ground black pepper
- 1 pinch cayenne pepper
- ½ cup mascarpone cheese
- 1 medium egg yolk
- ⅓ cup Parmesan cheese (grated)
- 1 (16 ounce) package round wonton wrappers
- 2 tablespoons butter
- 1 garlic clove (unpeeled)
- Fresh sage (chopped)
- 1 tablespoon Parmesan cheese (grated)

Instructions:

1. For the sauce: Melt the butter in a large pan, and when melted combine the flour until dissolved.

2. Stir in the Nutella followed by the cinnamon, nutmeg and whipping cream.

3. Blend until silky smooth and incorporated.

4. To make the ravioli filling: Add the cooked, mashed squash to a large bowl. Add the salt, together with the black and cayenne peppers. Stir in the mascarpone cheese, followed by the egg yolk and ⅓ cup of grated Parmesan, mixing well until the ravioli filling is combined and smooth.

5. Place a wonton wrapper on a clean countertop and run a damp finger along the outer edge of the wonton skin to lightly moisten.

6. Put approximately 1 teaspoon of the filling in the middle of the wonton and fold it in half to create a crescent shape, pressing the edges to seal. Repeat the process with the remaining wrappers.

7. Place a frying pan over moderate to low heat, and stir in the butter along with the unpeeled garlic clove.

8. In the meantime, bring a pan of lightly salted water to boil.

9. A few at a time, lower the filled ravioli into the boiling war, and cook until the ravioli float to the surface, around 2-3 minutes.

10. Drain and transfer the ravioli to the pan.

11. Increase the heat to moderate to high and cook until the filled ravioli is infused with garlic, 2-4 minutes.

12. Reheat the butternut squash sauce if necessary and pour over the ravioli.

13. Sprinkle with sage, black pepper, and grated cheese.

Recipe 22: Smoky Butternut Squash and Cacao Soup

This soup is in itself smoky, spicy and savory, but by adding a hint of Nutella sweetness, it is a flavor sensation. Enjoy with warm crusty bread for a satisfying meal or snack.

Serving Sizes: 4-6

Preparation Time: 15mins

Cook Time: 30mins

Total Cooking Time: 45mins

Ingredient List:

- 2 pounds butternut squash (peeled)
- 12 ounces fresh plum tomatoes (whole)
- ½ small onion (unpeeled)
- 4 garlic cloves (unpeeled)
- 1 canned chipotle in adobo
- ⅛ teaspoons ground allspice
- ⅛ teaspoons ground cinnamon
- ⅛ teaspoons fennel seeds
- 1 ounce cacao nibs
- 1 tablespoon extra virgin olive oil
- 1 tablespoon brown sugar
- 8 cups chicken stock
- 1 ounce Nutella
- Salt and pepper

HHHHHHHHHHHHHHHHHHHHHHHHHHHHHHHHHHHHHH

Instructions:

1. Using a tablespoon, scoop the seeds out of the squash, discard the seeds, and chop the flesh into 1" pieces, put in a small bowl and set to one side.

2. Heat a large pan or skillet over moderate heat.

3. Add the tomatoes, followed by the onion and garlic and roast, occasionally turning, until the tomatoes blister and the onion and garlic are charred, this will take around 8-10 minutes. Transfer the veggies, which will now have a smoky flavor, to a plate and set to one side to cool.

4. Carefully, remove the tomato's blistered parts and peel the onion and garlic.

5. Add the tomatoes, along with the onion and garlic to a food processor. Next, add the chipotle, ground allspice, ground cinnamon, fennel seeds and cacao nibs and blend to a smooth puree.

6. In a heavy pan over moderate heat, heat the olive oil until it sizzles.

7. Carefully add the puree and stir in the brown sugar, cook while continually stirring for 5 minutes.

8. Add the squash along with the chicken stock and bring to boil. Turn the heat down low, and cover with a lid. Simmer for 15-20 minutes, until the squash is fork tender. Remove the pan from the stove top.

9. Using a food blender or processor, in batches, puree the soup.

10. Using a fine strainer, puree the soup and using the back of a ladle, force it through. Throw away any solids.

11. In a pan, heat the strained soup over moderate heat.

12. Add the Nutella, continually stirring until it melts. Remove the pan from the heat and adjust the seasonings to taste.

13. Ladle the soup into bowls.

Recipe 23: Chicken Enchiladas with Nutella Mole Poblano

Love Mexican food but looking to shake things up? Then this Nutella infused mole sauce spooned on top of tasty chicken enchiladas is the dish for you!

Serving Sizes: 4

Preparation Time: 15mins

Cook Time: 20mins

Total Cooking Time: 35mins

Ingredient List:

Mole Sauce:

- ½ onion (chopped)
- 3 cloves garlic (chopped)
- ¼ cup hazelnuts
- ½ teaspoons salt
- ½ teaspoons cinnamon
- ½ teaspoons oregano
- ¼ teaspoons black pepper
- ¼ teaspoons cloves
- ¼ teaspoons cumin
- 3 ancho or chipotle chilies (stemmed, seeded, soaked in warm water)
- 1 (8 ounce) can tomato sauce (divided)
- ¼ cup Nutella
- ½ bar unsweetened dark chocolate
- 1 cup chicken stock

Enchiladas:

- 4 large flour tortillas
- 2 cups cooked chicken (shredded)
- To serve:
- ½ cup Mexican four-cheese blend
- 2 tablespoons sour cream + 1-2 teaspoons milk
- Sesame seeds

HHHHHHHHHHHHHHHHHHHHHHHHHHHHHHHHHHHH

Instructions:

1. In a medium-sized pan, sauté the onion and garlic until softened. Add the hazelnuts followed by the salt, cinnamon, oregano, black pepper, cloves, and cumin.

2. Drain and squeeze out the water from the chili peppers.

3. To a food processor, add the chili peppers, the onion mixture from the pan, and half of the tomato sauce. Process, adding additional tomato sauce if needed. The mixture should be smooth.

4. Return the mixture to the pan along with the remaining tomato sauce.

5. Add the Nutella followed by the dark chocolate.

6. On moderate to low heat, add approximately ½ cup of stock and stir to combine, adding additional broth as needed to achieve your preferred consistency.

7. Taste and adjust flavors to your preference. You may add additional Nutella or chocolate for a darker, richer mole.

8. As soon as the sauce is ready, reduce the heat to the lowest setting.

9. To a second pan, add 2-3 drizzles of oil and pan fry the tortillas until they are just pliable. Roll the enchiladas up with the shredded chicken and four cheese blends. Return briefly to the pan to fry to melt the cheese.

10. Arrange the enchiladas on a dinner plate and generously pour the mole over the top.

11. Lightly drizzle the sour cream on top of the mole.

12. Garnish with sesame seeds.

Recipe 24: Slow Cooker Black Bean Chilli with Nutella

A smokey, rich chili enhanced with the sweetness of Nutella, which also adds sweetness and depth.

Serving Sizes: 6

Preparation Time: 10mins

Cook Time: 7hours

Total Cooking Time: 7hours 10mins

Ingredient List:

- 1 tablespoon canola oil
- 1 yellow onion (peeled, chopped)
- 6 garlic cloves (minced)
- ¼ cup chili powder
- 1 tablespoon cumin
- 8 cups water
- 1 pound dried black beans
- 4 ounces canned green chilies (diced)
- ¼ cup flaked coconut
- 2 tablespoons Nutella
- 2 teaspoons dried oregano
- 2 teaspoons canned chilies in adobo sauce

HHHHHHHHHHHHHHHHHHHHHHHHHHHHHHHHHHHHH

Instructions:

1. Heat the oil in a slow cooker.

2. Add the remaining ingredients; the onion, garlic, chili powder, cumin, water, black beans, chilies, coconut, Nutella, oregano, and chilies.

3. Cook on a low heat for several hours, stirring every couple of hours until the black beans are tender.

4. Spoon into bowls and serve.

Recipe 25: Chicken Wings in Spicy Nutella Sauce

A sticky, sweet hot sauce makes these juicy chicken wings the ultimate finger-lickin' treat.

Serving Sizes: 4 (3 wings per serving)

Preparation Time: 15mins

Cook Time: 1hour

Total Cooking Time: 1hour 15mins

Ingredient List:

- Spicy Nutella Sauce:
- ¼ cup Nutella
- 2 tablespoons shredded toasted coconut
- ½ tablespoons coconut vinegar
- ½ tablespoons freshly squeezed lime juice
- ½ teaspoons hot sauce
- ¼ teaspoons each ginger and garlic paste
- Kosher salt

Chicken Wings:

- 12 raw chicken wings
- Handful fresh cilantro (roughly chopped)

HHHHHHHHHHHHHHHHHHHHHHHHHHHHHHHHHHHHHH

Instructions:

1. Mix together the Nutella, shredded coconut, vinegar, lime juice, hot sauce, pastes, and salt to taste. Set aside.

2. Preheat the main oven to 375 degrees F.

3. Place the chicken wings on a broiler pan and bake in the oven for just under half an hour. Turnover and bake for 20 more minutes.

4. Heat the grill to high and grill the wings until the skin crisps. Take out of the oven.

5. Heat the set-aside sauce in the microwave for 15-20 seconds until hot.

6. Toss the cooked wings in the hot BBQ sauce. Transfer to a serving plate and scatter with cilantro.

Recipe 26: Roast Duck with Hazelnut Mole

Roast duck and roasted hazelnuts are a marriage made in heaven, and this simple mole sauce will compliment an already amazing meal.

Serving Sizes: 6

Preparation Time: 15mins

Cook Time: 40mins

Total Cooking Time: 55mins

Ingredient List:

Hazelnut Mole:

- Water
- ½ cup Nutella
- 2 teaspoons garlic (peeled, minced)
- 1 teaspoon cayenne pepper

Roast Duck:

- 2 tablespoons butter
- 6 (7 ounce) duck breasts (fat scored in cross-hatch)
- 3½ ounces roasted hazelnuts (crushed)
- 1¾ ounces hazelnut oil
- 2 tablespoons sherry vinegar

HHHHHHHHHHHHHHHHHHHHHHHHHHHHHHHHHHHHH

Instructions:

1. First, make the Mole: In a pan slowly and a little at time, combine cold water with the Nutella and using an electric mixer, mix until creamy smooth. Add sufficient water to make the Nutella smooth but not too thin. If you do add too much water by mistake, add flour to thicken.

2. Add the garlic along with the cayenne pepper and continue to mix until combined.

3. Bring to a boil and cook until thick. Take off the heat but keep warm.

4. In an ovenproof skillet over moderate heat, melt the butter, add the duck breasts, skin side facing downwards over moderate to low heat, for 10-15 minutes, or until the skin is crisp, and the fat rendered.

5. Drain away the fat.

6. Place the skillet in the oven, still keeping the breasts facing skin side down, and roast for 3-4 minutes, until the duck is medium to rare. Transfer to a plate and keep warm.

7. Wipe the pan clean and add the roasted hazelnuts along with the hazelnut oil. Continually stirring over a high heat for 60 seconds, to lightly toast.

8. Deglaze the pan with sherry vinegar, then add the hazelnut mole and simmer for a couple of minutes.

9. Slice the duck and transfer to dinner plates, drizzle the mole over the top and serve.

Recipe 27: Chili Chinese Chicken with Nutella

Nutella adds a new and exciting flavor to this spiced curry.

Serving Sizes: 3-4

Preparation Time: 10mins

Cook Time: 30mins

Total Cooking Time: 40mins

Ingredient List:

- 8-9 ounces boneless, skinless chicken (chopped)
- 1 teaspoon cornflour mixed with 1 tablespoon water and a pinch salt
- Canola oil
- 2 cloves garlic (finely chopped)
- ¼ teaspoons fresh ginger (peeled, grated)
- 1 yellow onion (finely chopped)
- 2 teaspoons tomato puree
- Pinch turmeric
- ½ teaspoons garam masala
- 1 teaspoon granulated sugar
- ½ teaspoons chilli powder
- 1½ teaspoons soy sauce
- 4 teaspoons Nutella
- 2 tablespoons scallions (finely chopped)
- Small handful fresh cilantro (chopped)

HHHHHHHHHHHHHHHHHHHHHHHHHHHHHHHHHHHHH

Instructions:

1. Toss the chicken pieces in the cornstarch mixture until coated.

2. Pour enough canola oil into a saucepan to deep fry the chicken. When hot, fry the chicken until cooked and golden, set to one side.

3. In a nonstick kadai, heat a little more oil over moderately high heat.

4. Add the garlic, ginger, and onion, sauté for a couple of minutes before adding the tomato puree, turmeric, garam masala, sugar, and chili powder. Stir well and cook for a few minutes

5. Add the soy sauce, stir and cook for 60 seconds.

6. Turn the heat to low and place the chicken back in the pan along with the Nutella. Cook, while stirring, for 3-4 minutes.

7. Sprinkle in the scallions and cilantro, stir well and spoon into bowls.

8. Enjoy!

Recipe 28: Raspberry, Brie and Nutella Waffle Panini

An indulgent panini made with Belgian waffles, gooey brie, fresh raspberries and rich Nutella. The ultimate in comfort food!

Serving Sizes: 1-2

Preparation Time: 4mins

Cook Time: 6mins

Total Cooking Time: 10mins

Ingredient List:

- 2 large Belgian waffles
- 5 tablespoons Nutella
- 4 ounces fresh raspberries
- 4 ounces brie cheese (thinly sliced)
- Confectioner's sugar (for dusting)

HHHHHHHHHHHHHHHHHHHHHHHHHHHHHHHHHHHHH

Instructions:

1. Spread each waffle with Nutella.

2. On one waffle, arrange the raspberries, on the other arrange the sliced Brie. Sandwich the two waffles together so that the fillings are in the middle, touching.

3. Over a moderately high heat, place a medium-sized skillet. Place the waffle sandwich in the pan and cook for a few minutes each side until the cheese melts.

4. Dust with confectioner's sugar, slice in half and serve!

Recipe 29: Chocolate Cupcakes with Nutella Ganache and Bacon

Rich chocolate cupcakes with a hazelnut-infused ganache sprinkled with bacon bits are sure to impress family and friends.

Serving Sizes: 12

Preparation Time: 15mins

Cook Time: 25mins

Total Cooking Time: 40mins

Ingredient List:

Cupcakes:

- ¾ cup cocoa powder
- 2 cups all-purpose flour
- 1 cup white sugar
- 1 cups brown sugar
- 2 teaspoons bicarb of soda
- 1 teaspoon baking powder
- ½ teaspoons kosher salt
- 2 medium eggs (lightly beaten)
- 1 cup strong brewed coffee (cold)
- 1 cup whole milk
- ½ cup vegetable oil
- 12 strips crispy streaky bacon (cooked, crumbled)
- Nutella Ganache:
- ¼ cup whipping cream
- 2 ounces baking chocolate buttons
- ¼ cup Nutella

HHHHHHHHHHHHHHHHHHHHHHHHHHHHHHHHHHHHH

Instructions:

1. Preheat the main oven to 380 degrees F. Grease a 12-cup muffin tins.

2. In a large mixing bowl, sift the cocoa powder, all-purpose flour, white and brown sugar, bicarb of soda, baking powder, and salt.

3. In another bowl combine the eggs along with the strong brewed coffee, whole milk, and vegetable oil.

4. Slowly add the liquid ingredient mixture to the dry ingredients and mix to combine, without using a mixer.

5. As soon as the texture is silky smooth fold in 75% of the cooked and crumbled bacon. Next, pour the batter into the prepared muffin tin.

6. Bake in the oven for 25 minutes.

7. When sufficiently baked remove the muffin tin from the oven and allow to cool.

8. When cool, remove from the muffin tins and place on baking rack.

9. Next, prepare the ganache: In a microwave-safe bowl, combine the whipping cream with the chocolate buttons and Nutella, Heat in 10-15 second intervals, stir until silky smooth.

10. Place the ganache in a piping bag and swirl over the cooled cupcakes.

11. While the ganache is still soft, scatter with the crumbled bacon.

Recipe 30: Paprika and Hazelnut Chocolate Cookies

These sophisticated, grownup cookies combine crunchy toasted hazelnuts, Spanish smoked paprika, and Nutella for a flavor sensation.

Serving Sizes: 25

Preparation Time: 15mins

Cook Time: 10mins

Total Cooking Time: 25mins

Ingredient List:

- 1 cup flour
- ½ cup granulated sugar
- 2 teaspoons sweet Spanish smoked paprika (divided)
- ⅛ teaspoons sea salt
- 2 large eggs
- 1 cup Nutella (room temperature)
- ½ cup hazelnut (skinned, toasted, coarsely chopped)
- 1 tablespoon powdered sugar (to dust)
- Flaky sea salt

HHHHHHHHHHHHHHHHHHHHHHHHHHHHHHHHHHHHHH

.

Instructions:

1. Preheat the main oven to 350 degrees F. Cover 2 baking sheets with parchment.

2. In a mixing bowl, combine the flour together with the sugar, 1½ teaspoons of smoked paprika, and the ⅛ teaspoons of sea salt.

3. Using a wooden spoon, add the eggs and mix to form a dough. Add the Nutella followed by the hazelnuts, working the mixture to form a smooth dough, mixing for a maximum of 2 minutes.

4. Evenly divide the dough into 25 equally sized portions and using the palms of your hands roll the portions into balls.

5. Arrange the balls, 2" apart, on the baking sheets and one sheet at a time put back in the center of the oven for 8-10 minutes, or until the cookies are crisp, spread, and have a few cracks on top.

6. While the cookies are warm, sprinkle with the remaining ½ teaspoons of smoked paprika, the powdered sugar, and flakes of sea salt.

Recipe 31: Chocolate Hazelnut Toasts with Salted Balsamic Strawberries

Balsamic strawberries and Nutella are a match made in heaven. The perfect weekend brunch treat.

Serving Sizes: 4

Preparation Time: 10mins

Cook Time: 5mins

Total Cooking Time: 15mins

Ingredient List:

- 2 tablespoons balsamic vinegar
- 2 teaspoons granulated sugar
- 1 tablespoon dark brown sugar
- 4 –5 ounces strawberries (sliced)
- Pinch of salt
- 4 slices rye bread
- Crushed hazelnuts (to top)

HHHHHHHHHHHHHHHHHHHHHHHHHHHHHHHHHHHHHHH

Instructions:

1. Combine the vinegar with the sugars in a medium bowl, and whisk. Add the strawberries, stirring to combine and sprinkle with a pinch of salt. Allow this mixture to steep for a maximum of 10 minutes.

2. Using a mesh strainer, strain the balsamic strawberries and pat dry using a kitchen paper towel.

3. Toast the rye bread to your level of crispness.

4. Next, spread lashings of Nutella onto each slice of toast. Top with the balsamic strawberries. Scatter with crushed hazelnuts and serve!

Recipe 32: Nutty Garbanzo Bean Hummus

This recipe is a nuttier alternative to regular hummus.

Serving Sizes: 3 cups

Preparation Time: 4mins

Cook Time: N/A

Total Cooking Time: 4mins

Ingredient List:

- 16 ounces canned garbanzo beans (drained, rinsed)
- 1 tablespoon tahini
- ½ cup Nutella
- ¼ cup olive oil
- Graham crackers and veggies (for dipping)

HHHHHHHHHHHHHHHHHHHHHHHHHHHHHHHHHHHHHH

Instructions:

1. Add the beans, tahini, Nutella, and olive oil to a food blender and process until creamy.

2. Serve with graham crackers or raw veggies to dip.

Recipe 33: Coffee and Hazelnut Marinated Steak

The great thing about this marinade is most of the ingredients are already in your store cupboards.

Serving Sizes: 2

Preparation Time: 15mins

Cook Time: 15mins

Total Cooking Time: 8hours 30mins

Ingredient List:

- ¼ cup onion (peeled, chopped)
- 1 tablespoon Nutella
- 2 tablespoons extra virgin olive oil
- ¼ cup instant espresso (brewed, cold)
- Freshly squeezed lemon juice from ½ lemon
- ½ teaspoons cayenne pepper
- ½ teaspoons cumin
- 2 strip steaks

HHHHHHHHHHHHHHHHHHHHHHHHHHHHHHHHHHHHHH

Instructions:

1. In a pan over moderate to high heat. Sauté the onions for 2-3 minutes.

2. In a food processor, mix the Nutella along with the olive oil, instant brewed coffee, fried onions, freshly squeezed lemon juice, cayenne pepper, and cumin. Mix together until incorporated.

3. Transfer the mixture to a ziplock bag along with the strip steaks and marinate overnight.

4. Place the strip steak on a grill and cook for 5 minutes on one side, flip over, and cook for 4 minutes on the reverse.

5. Serve, drizzled with the leftover marinade.

Recipe 34: Nutella Chili Sloppy Joe

Nutella adds a sweet twist to this iconic savory American favorite.

Serving Sizes: 4

Preparation Time: 5mins

Cook Time: 10mins

Total Cooking Time: 15mins

Ingredient List:

- 4 buns (split in half)
- 8½ ounces chorizo (finely chopped)
- 17 ounces minced beef
- Salt and black pepper (to taste)
- Barbecue rub (to taste)
- 3 tablespoons olive oil
- 1 onion (peeled, diced)
- 2 garlic cloves (peeled, chopped)
- 2 tablespoons tomato paste
- 1 ounce white wine
- Splash of balsamic vinegar
- 4 Thai chilies (cut into fine rings)
- 1 tablespoon Nutella
- 1 wasabi (grated)

HHHHHHHHHHHHHHHHHHHHHHHHHHHHHHHHHHHHH

Instructions:

1. Preheat a grill with a cast iron pan.

2. First, roast the buns to get charred grill marks, and once sufficiently charred put to one side.

3. In a large mixing bowl, combine the chorizo, minced beef, salt, black pepper, barbecue rub and mix to incorporate.

4. In a pan, heat the oil and sauté the onions, add the garlic and continue to sauté until the onions are translucent. Once browned, add the tomato paste, white wine, balsamic vinegar and stir to combine.

5. As soon as the mixture is sufficiently cooked, add the meat mixture and roast for between 15-20 minutes.

6. Add the chilies and roast for an additional 1-2 minutes.

7. Stir in the Nutella and mix to combine.

8. Evenly spread the mixture over the bottom part of the buns.

9. Spread the grated wasabi over the top, inner side of the top bun.

Recipe 35: Cornbread Waffles with Pulled Pork and Nutella BBQ Sauce

A sweet and savory relish that will give your grilled food the wow factor.

Serving Sizes: 4-6

Preparation Time: 10mins

Cook Time: 20mins

Total Cooking Time: 30mins

Ingredient List:

BBQ Sauce:

- 2 tablespoons American mustard
- 1 tablespoon Nutella
- 1 tablespoon hot sauce
- 1 tablespoon sherry vinegar

Waffles:

- 1 (8½ ounce) box cornbread mix
- 1¼ cups whole milk
- 2 tablespoons salted butter (melted)
- 2 medium eggs
- ¾ cup Cheddar cheese (grated)
- Nonstick spray
- 2 cups leftover pulled pork
- ¼ cup green onions (diced)

HHHHHHHHHHHHHHHHHHHHHHHHHHHHHHHHHHHHH

Instructions:

1. Whisk together the mustard, Nutella, hot sauce, and vinegar. Set aside until ready to serve.

2. Preheat the main oven to 200 degrees F. Cover a cookie sheet with a wire rack, set to one side.

3. Preheat a waffle iron.

4. In a mixing bowl, combine the cornbread mix, whole milk, melted butter, eggs, and grated Cheddar.

5. Spritz the waffle iron with nonstick spray.

6. Cook the waffle batter in the iron according to manufacturer's directions.

7. Place the cooked waffles on the wire rack. Pop in the oven to keep them warm.

8. Reheat the pulled pork until hot through and arrange it on top of waffles.

9. Serve with the set-aside BBQ sauce.

Recipe 36: Nutty Bacon and Cheese Beef Burger with Caramelized Onions

The ultimate man burger, juicy grass-fed beef patties, melting gooey cheese, caramelized onion and a drizzle of Nutella.

Serving Sizes: 4

Preparation Time: 20mins

Cook Time: 30mins

Total Cooking Time: 50mins

Ingredient List:

- 1 pound grass fed ground beef
- 1 teaspoon salt
- ½ teaspoons pepper
- 1 medium egg
- ⅛ cup almond flour
- ½ tablespoons olive oil
- 4 slices sharp cheddar cheese
- ½ tablespoons butter
- 1–2 sweet onions (peeled, sliced)
- ½ cup Nutella
- 1 teaspoon garlic powder
- 8 slices bacon
- 4 brioche buns (split in half)

HHHHHHHHHHHHHHHHHHHHHHHHHHHHHHHHHHHHH

Instructions:

1. In a mixing bowl, combine the beef with the salt, pepper, egg and almond flour. Using clean hands form the mixture into 4 generous meatballs.

2. In a cast iron skillet over moderate heat add the olive oil. When hot, add the meatballs to the skillet and with the back of a wooden spoon flatten to form a patty.

3. Flip the patties over and season with more salt and pepper.

4. Cook the patties to your desired level of doneness.

5. When the meat is nearly cooked to your liking top each pattie, while still in the skillet with a slice of cheese and allow to melt.

6. To caramelize the onions, heat a frying pan over moderate heat and add the butter along with a drop of olive oil. Swirl the pan to ensure that it is evenly coated. As soon as the butter begins to sizzle, add the onions, stirring to ensure that the onions are coated with the butter and oil.

7. Reduce the heat and continue cooking until browned. Add additional butter if needed to prevent burning.

8. In a separate small pan cook the bacon to your desired level of doneness.

9. Toast the brioche buns until golden brown on both sides.

10. While the buns are toasting, add the Nutella to a microwave-safe bowl and in 30-second intervals, microwave until melted.

11. Assemble the buns by placing a cheese beef burger on the bottom inner half of 4 buns, top with bacon and onions. Drizzle the melted Nutella over the onions and top with the upper slice of bun to form a sandwich.

Recipe 37: Hazelnut Spread & Olive Oil Bruschetta

A tasty supper time snack or nibble.

Serving Sizes: 6-8

Preparation Time: 2mins

Cook Time: 3mins

Total Cooking Time: 5mins

Ingredient List:

- 1 crusty French baguette (cut into 2" slices)
- Nutella (as required)
- Extra Virgin olive oil (to drizzle)

HHHHHHHHHHHHHHHHHHHHHHHHHHHHHHHHHHHHHHH

Instructions:

1. Toast the bread slices until golden brown.

2. Spread each of the slices of French baguette with lashings of Nutella and drizzle with extra virgin olive oil.

Recipe 38: Nutella Apple n' Cheese Sandwich

Sometimes the simplest things are the best, and this sandwich is an ideal after-school snack.

Serving Sizes: 2

Preparation Time: 1mins

Cook Time: 3mins

Total Cooking Time: 4mins

Ingredient List:

- 4 slices brown bread
- 2 teaspoons Nutella
- ½ Granny Smith apple (cored, thinly sliced)
- 2 slices low-fat Cheddar cheese

HHHHHHHHHHHHHHHHHHHHHHHHHHHHHHHHHHHHH

Instructions:

1. Spread each slice of bread with Nutella and top with 2-3 slices of apple.

2. Top with a cheese slice followed by another slice of brown bread.

3. Heat a pan, and lightly cook the sandwiches until crisp and lightly golden on both sides.

Recipe 39: Loaded Sweet Potato Fries

Next time you whip up a batch of crispy and delicious sweet potato fries, ditch the ketchup and mayo. Instead, reach for the Nutella and peanut butter! You can thank us later.

Serving Sizes: 6

Preparation Time: 15mins

Cook Time: 30mins

Total Cooking Time: 45mins

Ingredient List:

- 5 large sweet potatoes (scrubbed, chopped into 'fries')
- 2½ tablespoons olive oil
- 1 teaspoon salt
- ¼ cup organic smooth peanut butter
- ¼ cup Nutella
- 2 tablespoons mixed roasted nuts (chopped)

HHHHHHHHHHHHHHHHHHHHHHHHHHHHHHHHHHHHH

Instructions:

1. Preheat the main oven to 450 degrees F.

2. Toss the potato fries with olive oil and salt. Spread out over baking sheets in single layers.

3. Bake in the oven for just over half an hour, flipping halfway through cooking.

4. Take out of the oven and sprinkle with more salt. Allow to cool a little before transferring to a serving plate.

5. Place the peanut butter and Nutella in separate small bowls. Add a few drops of water to each. Stir and microwave for 10-15 seconds, until runny.

6. Drizzle the peanut butter and Nutella over the fries then sprinkle with the chopped nuts.

7. Enjoy!

About the Author

Angel Burns learned to cook when she worked in the local seafood restaurant near her home in Hyannis Port in Massachusetts as a teenager. The head chef took Angel under his wing and taught the young woman the tricks of the trade for cooking seafood. The skills she had learned at a young age helped her get accepted into Boston University's Culinary Program where she also minored in business administration.

Summers off from school meant working at the same restaurant but when Angel's mentor and friend retired as head chef, she took over after graduation and created classic and new dishes that delighted the diners. The restaurant flourished under Angel's culinary creativity and one customer developed more than an appreciation for Angel's food. Several months after taking over the position, the young woman met her future husband at work and they have been inseparable ever since. They still live in Hyannis Port with their two children and a cocker spaniel named Buddy.

Angel Burns turned her passion for cooking and her business acumen into a thriving e-book business. She has authored several successful books on cooking different types of dishes using simple ingredients for novices and experienced chefs alike. She is still head chef in Hyannis Port and says she will probably never leave!

♥ ♭ ♥ ♥ ♥ ♥ ♭ ◄ ♭ ♥ ♥ ♥ ♥ ♥ ♭ ◄ ♭ ♥ ♭ ♥ ♥ ♥ ♭ ◄ ♥

Author's Afterthoughts

With so many books out there to choose from, I want to thank you for choosing this one and taking precious time out of your life to buy and read my work. Readers like you are the reason I take such passion in creating these books.

It is with gratitude and humility that I express how honored I am to become a part of your life and I hope that you take the same pleasure in reading this book as I did in writing it.

Can I ask one small favour? I ask that you write an honest and open review on Amazon of what you thought of the book. This will help other readers make an informed choice on whether to buy this book.

My sincerest thanks,

Angel Burns

If you want to be the first to know about news, new books, events and giveaways, subscribe to my newsletter by clicking the link below

https://angel-burns.gr8.com

or Scan QR-code

Made in the USA
Middletown, DE
01 February 2020